Chadwick Library Edition

*

Selected Written Works of Rudolf Steiner

Vol. 6

# A PATH TO SELF-KNOWLEDGE

*In Eight Meditations*

RUDOLF STEINER

# A PATH TO SELF-KNOWLEDGE

## IN EIGHT MEDITATIONS

*Translated by*
Julia Selg *and* Thomas O'Keefe

CHADWICK LIBRARY EDITION

New York, New York

2019

COPYRIGHT INFORMATION



Chadwick Library Edition is an imprint of
SteinerBooks (Anthroposophic Press)
214 W 29th Street, Suite 2D, New York, NY 10001 USA
www.steinerbooks.org



Translation by Julia Selg and
Thomas O'Keefe, with reference to an earlier
translation by Christopher Bamford.

This book comprises volume 16 in the Collected
Works (CW) of Rudolf Steiner. It is a translation of
*Ein Weg zur Selbsterkenntnis des Menschen:
In acht Meditationen*, published by
Rudolf Steiner Verlag, Dornach, Switzerland, 2004.

ISBN 978-1-7324613-7-6 (Trade Edition)
978-1-7324613-6-9 (Limited Edition)



Printed in Verona, Italy

# TABLE OF CONTENTS
Vol. 6

# INTRODUCTORY REMARKS

The aim of this book is to provide spiritual-scientific findings concerning the nature and essence of the human being. The presentation is organized to allow the reader to grow into what is presented in such a way that in the course of his reading it becomes for him like a conversation with himself. If this inner conversation then forms itself in such a way that previously concealed inner forces, which can be awakened in every soul, reveal themselves, then reading this book can lead to real inner soul-work. And the soul may gradually find itself impelled to undertake a process of soul-journeying that truly brings it into a seeing of the spiritual world. For this reason, what is to be imparted is presented in the form of eight meditations that can really be carried out. If this happens, then these meditations can be well suited to transmit to the soul, through the soul's own inner deepening, what is spoken of in them.

The attempt has been made, on one hand, to provide something of interest to the reader who is already thoroughly familiar with the literature and work in the realm of the suprasensory as it is here understood. Thus, through the character of what is presented, and because it is conveyed in a way that is directly connected to the soul's experience, the knower of suprasensory life may perhaps find something here that seems important to him. On the other hand, many readers can find that a person who still stands at a distance from the results of spiritual science can also benefit especially from a presentation such as this.

This book is intended to supplement and expand upon my other writings on spiritual science. Yet it can also be read independently.

In my book *Theosophy* and in my *Outline of Occult Science*,[1] I strove to present things as they are revealed to observation directed toward the spiritual. The mode of presentation in these works is a descriptive one, whose progression was determined by the lawfulness revealed from out of the things themselves. –[2] In this *Path to Self-Knowledge*, the mode of presentation is different. It tells of what a soul can experience when it sets out on the path to the spirit in a certain way. This book may therefore be regarded as the reporting of soul experiences. One should bear in mind, however, that the experiences that can be gained in the way described here will have to take on a specific form in every individual soul, depending on the soul's unique character. The goal has been to do justice to this fact, so that one can also imagine that what is described here has been lived through, just as presented, by one particular soul. (It is for this reason that I have called these meditations "*A* Path to Self-Knowledge.") Precisely for this reason, this book may also enable other souls to live into what is here described and achieve corresponding aims. Thus, this book supplements and amplifies what may be found in my book *Knowledge of the Higher Worlds: How Is It Achieved?*[3]

Only a few basic spiritual-scientific experiences are presented. For the time being, the author does not envision any further communications of this nature regarding other aspects of "spiritual science."

RUDOLF STEINER
*Munich, August 1912*

# FIRST MEDITATION

## *The meditant attempts to gain a true inner picture of the physical body*[4]

When the soul, through the senses and through its own activity of inner picturing (*Vorstellen*), is given over to the phenomena of the outer world, it cannot, upon true self-reflection, say that it perceives those phenomena or that it experiences the things of the outer world. For in truth, as long as the soul is given over to the outer world, it is not aware of itself. The sunlight spreading out in space from things in a manifold color phenomenon: that is what actually experiences itself in the soul. When the soul rejoices in some event, the soul itself – in that moment of rejoicing – *is* joy, insofar as it is aware of the matter. The joy experiences itself in the soul. The soul is *one* with its experience of the world. It does not experience itself *as* something that rejoices, admires, delights, or fears. It *is* joy, admiration, delight, fear. If the soul were always to admit this, then those periods of time in which it steps back from its experience with the outer world and reflects upon itself would appear to it in their proper light. They would appear as a very special kind of life – one that, for the time being, cannot at all be compared to ordinary soul life. With this special kind of life, the riddles of the soul's existence first begin to emerge into consciousness. And these riddles are essentially the source of all other world riddles. – The outer world and the inner world present themselves to the human spirit when, for shorter or longer periods, the soul ceases to be *one* with the outer world and withdraws itself into the solitude of its own being.

This withdrawing, however, is not a simple process that, once accomplished, can be repeated in more or less the same way. It is, rather, the beginning of a journey into previously unknown worlds. Once one has begun the journey, each step one takes opens the way to further steps. Each step is also the preparation for these further steps and makes the soul capable of taking them. And with each step, one learns more about the answer to the question, "What is the human being in the true sense of the word?" Worlds hidden from ordinary reflection on life now break open. And yet, what can reveal the truth about this reflection on life lies only in these hidden worlds. – Even though no answer is all-encompassing and final, the answers that can be earned through this inner soul-journeying far surpass what the senses and the sense-bound intellect are able to provide. And the human being has need of something other than what is given by the senses and the sense-bound intellect. He will realize that this is so when he truly reflects upon himself.

First of all, it is necessary to begin this journeying with sober, dry considerations. They provide a reliable point of departure for penetrating deeper into those suprasensory realms that are the soul's ultimate concern. Many a soul wishes to spare itself this starting point and would like to enter directly into the suprasensory. But a healthy soul – even though it may initially seek to avoid such considerations due to an aversion to them – will later give itself over to them. For no matter how much one may have learned about the suprasensory from another starting point, it is only through considerations such as the following that one will be on firm ground.

Moments may arise in the life of the soul in which the soul will speak to itself as follows: You must be able to withdraw from everything an outer world can give you if you do not wish to be forced into a confession that you cannot live with: namely, that you are a mere self-experiencing absurdity. – What you perceive outside of yourself is there without you. It was in existence without you, and it will be in existence without you. Why do colors perceive themselves within you if your perceiving is so insignificant to them? Why do the substances and forces of the outer world form your body? Your body enlivens itself into your outer appearance. The outer world, reshaping itself, becomes you. You become aware that you need this body. For without your senses, which only your body can equip you with, you would be, for the time being, utterly incapable of experiencing anything within yourself. You would be – as you are at your present state of development – empty without your body. The body gives you inner fullness and content. – And then all those reflections can arise without which a human existence cannot endure if it is not at certain times – in moments that will inevitably occur in the life of every human being – to fall into unbearable contradiction with itself. This body is now alive in such a way that it is the expression of the soul's experiencing. Its processes are such that the soul lives through the body and experiences itself in it. One day, that will not be so. What lives in the body will then be subject to quite different laws than it is now when the processes that live in the body proceed on behalf of my soul's experiencing. What lives in the body will be subject to the laws according to which the substances and forces in outer nature act – laws that have nothing more to do with me or my life. The body, to which I owe my soul's experiences, will then be absorbed into the general course of the world and will act there in a way that no longer has anything in common with what I experience in myself.

A consideration of this kind can bring before one's inner experience all the horror of the thought of death, but without intermingling any of the purely personal feelings that the soul usually connects with this thought. Such feelings make it so that the calm, composed mood required for insightful consideration will not easily arise to meet this thought. – It is all too understandable that the human being wishes to gain knowledge about death and about a life of the soul independent of the dissolution of the body. But the attitude he assumes toward the questions that come into consideration here – almost more so than in relation to any other question in the world – tends to obscure a factual view of things, prompting him to accept as valid those answers that are supplied by his wishes. However, there is no way to obtain true insight into something in the spiritual realm about which one cannot, with a completely impartial attitude, accept a "no" just as willingly as a "yes." And one need only look conscientiously within oneself to see clearly that one would not accept with the same equanimity the knowledge that with the death of the body the life of the soul is also extinguished, as one would the opposite: a knowledge that finds evidence of the soul's continued existence after death. Certainly there are people who believe quite honestly that with the dissolution of the bodily life, the soul too is annihilated – and who, once they have accepted this thought, have managed to live with it. Yet, even for such people, it is nevertheless the case that they are by no means unbiased in their feelings with regard to such thoughts. In spite of all the horrors of annihilation, they do not allow the desire for continued existence to speak louder in them than the reasons that make a strong case for their final conclusion. To that extent, the inner pictures of such people are often more objective than those of others who, without being aware of it, delude themselves or allow themselves to be deluded about the reasons for this continuity of life because in the secret depths of their souls there burns a desire for such a continued life. Yet, the degree of bias among the deniers of immortality is no less than it is among believers. It is only different in nature. Among such deniers are some who form a definite inner picture of what are known as life and existence. This inner picture then leads them to need to think of certain conditions that must hold true in order for this life to be possible. Thus, when they now consider existence in this way, it becomes apparent to them that the conditions necessary for soul life can no longer be present when the body falls away. Such people do not notice that it was they who first formed a particular inner picture of the only possible way life could be – and that they cannot believe that life continues after death only because the inner picture they have formed provides no possibility for conceiving of a body-free existence. They are not in fact biased by their wishes but by their inner pictures from which they now cannot break free. There are still many other ways to succumb to bias in this realm. One can only give particular examples of all that exists in this sense.

The thought that one day the body, through whose processes the soul expresses itself, will become part of the outer world and follow laws that bear no relationship to inner experience, allows the experience of death to arise in the soul in such a way that no wish or personal interest need interfere with one's reflection. It will arise in such a way that this experience can lead to a pure, impersonal question of knowledge. But then, as a result, the feeling will soon occur that the thought of death is important not so much for its own sake, but rather because it can shed light upon life. One will be forced to arrive at the view that the riddle of life is to be understood through the nature of death.

The fact that the soul longs for its own continuance should by all means incite the soul to be wary of every opinion it forms regarding this continuance. For why should the facts of the world be concerned with what the soul feels? Because of the nature of its needs, the soul may feel itself to be meaningless when forced to think that it could flare up like a flame from fuel out of the substance of its body and then be extinguished again. It could indeed be so, even if it would be felt to be meaningless. – When the soul turns its gaze toward the body, it should take into account only what the body can reveal to it. In so doing, it appears as if laws are at work in nature that bring substances and forces into a process of interplay – and as if these laws govern the body and, after a certain period of time, reintegrate it into the universal process of interplay.

One may turn this thought any way one wishes: one will find that it is certainly useful in natural science but proves entirely impossible when applied to true reality. One can find that this thought alone is scientifically clear and sober, and all others are only subjective belief; one can certainly persuade oneself of this. But if one is truly unbiased, one cannot adhere to this thought. And that is what matters. For what should be considered is not what the soul, by its nature, perceives to be important, but only what is revealed by the outer world, from which the body is taken. After death, this outer world integrates into itself the substances and forces of the human body. In the outer world, these substances and forces then follow laws that are entirely indifferent to what happens in the human body during life. These laws (which are physical and chemical in nature) relate to the body no differently than to any other lifeless thing in the outer world. It is impossible to think anything other than that this indifferent relationship of the outer world to the human body arises not just after death, but that it already exists during life. It is not on the basis of what derives from life that one can gain an inner picture of the sensory outer world's share in the human body. Rather, one can do so only by thinking to oneself as follows: "All that you have with you as the bearer of your senses, as the mediator of the processes through which your soul lives, will be dealt with by the world you perceive in a way that becomes evident to you when you let your conception wander beyond the limits of your life – a conception that takes into account that a time will come when you will no longer have with you that within which you now experience yourself." Every other inner picture of the relationship of the sensory outer world to the body, when considered in the light of reality, can be felt of its own accord to be untenable. But the inner picture that it is only after death that the outer world's share in the body really becomes evident does not conflict with what is genuinely experienced in the outer and inner worlds. The soul feels nothing unbearable in the thought that the body's substances and forces fall under the sway of the processes of the outer world, which themselves have nothing to do with the soul's own life. When devoting itself to life in a completely unbiased way, the soul cannot discover in its depths any wish arising from the body that would make the thought of the body's dissolution after death uncomfortable. The situation becomes unbearable only if the inner picture were to be formed that the substances and forces that return to the outer world take the self-experiencing soul with them. Such an inner picture would be unbearable for the very same reason as would any other that does not follow naturally from devotion to what is revealed by the outer world.

To ascribe to the outer world an entirely different share in the body's existence during life than it has after death is a thought based on nothing. As a senseless thought, it must always bounce back from an encounter with reality, whereas the thought that the outer world has the same share in the body during life as it does after death is quite healthy. When considering the latter thought, the soul feels itself entirely in harmony with what the facts reveal. It can sense that this inner picture does *not* bring it into disharmony with the facts, which speak for themselves and to which no artificial thoughts need to be added.

One does not always pay attention to how beautifully the soul's natural, healthy feeling harmonizes with what nature reveals. This fact might appear so self-evident that it hardly merits any special attention; and yet, this apparently insignificant fact sheds light upon our question. There is nothing unbearable in the thought that the physical body will dissolve into the elements; but the thought that this could also happen to the soul seems senseless. There are many human, personal reasons that make this seem senseless; objective examination must leave these out of consideration. A wholly impersonal devotion to what the outer world teaches us shows that the share in the soul ascribed to the outer world during life can in fact be no different than it is after death. The decisive point is that this thought arises as a necessity and can resist all possible objections that one can raise against it. Whoever thinks this thought with full consciousness will feel this as a matter of direct certainty. In truth, this is how both those who believe in immortality and those who deny it actually think. The latter may well also claim that the laws that are active in the body after death also contain the conditions for the bodily processes during life. But they are wrong to *believe* that they are really capable of imagining that these laws behave differently in relation to the body as carrier of the soul during life than they do in relation to the body after death.

The only inner picture possible in itself is that this special composition of forces, which manifests itself in and through the body, relates to the body in the body's capacity as carrier of the soul in the very same way – that is, without having a share in this soul-carrying capacity – as does the composition of forces which brings about the processes in the dead body. It is not that the soul has no share in the body in the context of the body's capacity as soul-carrier, but rather that the substances and forces of the body have none. The soul experiences itself in the encounter with the body; but the body lives *with* the outer world, *in* it, and *through* it. And the body allows the processes in the soul to be decisive for it in just the same way as it does the processes of the outer world. One must come to the view that, for the circulation of the blood within the body, the warmth and coldness of the outer world are just as influential as the fear or the sense of shame that take place in the soul.

Thus, first of all, one feels the laws of the outer world active within oneself in the particular composition of substances and forces that manifests itself in the formation of the human body.

One feels this body to be a member of the outer world. But one remains a stranger to its inner coherence. In our times, outer science clarifies to some extent how the laws of the outer world unite in the entirely extraordinary being that presents itself as the human body. It is to be hoped that, in the future, this knowledge will continue to advance. But the progress of such knowledge cannot in the least bit change how the soul must think of its relationship to the body. On the contrary, it will come to show more and more clearly that the laws of the outer world relate to the soul in exactly the same way before death as they do after death. It is an illusion to expect that, as knowledge of nature advances, the laws of the outer world will produce evidence as to the exact way in which soul life is based on bodily processes. One will discern with increasing precision what occurs in the body during life; but in the end, the soul will always feel these processes as external to itself in the same way as the processes in the body after death.

Consequently, within the outer world, the body must appear as an autonomous composition of forces and substances that is explicable within its own confines as a member of this outer world. – Nature lets the plant come into being; it dissolves it again. Nature governs the human body and lets it pass away within nature's being. When the human being confronts nature in the light of such a consideration, he will be able to forget *himself* and all that is in him, and to perceive his body as a member of the outer world that he has with him. If he thinks in this way about his relationship to himself and to nature, then he will experience as something he has with him what can be called one's *physical body*.

## SECOND MEDITATION

### *The meditant attempts to gain a true inner picture of the elemental or etheric body*

The soul can be driven into complete uncertainty regarding its own being by the conception that it must form as a consequence of the fact of death. This will be the case if the soul believes it cannot know of any world other than the sensory world and what the intellect is able to know about this world. Ordinary soul life looks upon the physical body. Soul life sees this body pass over after death into the context of nature, which has no share in what the soul experienced as its own existence before death. It may certainly know (through the previous meditation) that during life the physical body stands in the same relationship to the soul as it does after death; but this insight takes the soul no further than to the recognition of the inner independence of its own experiencing up until the moment of death. What happens to the physical body after death is shown to the soul through observation of the outer world. There is no such observation of what happens to inner experiencing after death. Soul life, as it is, cannot look beyond the boundary of death. If a soul is unable to form inner pictures extending beyond the world that absorbs the body after death, then it is also impossible for it to see, after death, anything other than empty nothingness in relation to everything of a soul nature.

For that to change, the soul must perceive the outer world with means other than the senses and sense-bound intellect. These both belong to the body and perish with it. What they say can never lead to anything other than what results from the first meditation. And what results from it is that the soul can admit to itself: "You are bound to your body. This body is subject to natural laws that stand in the same relationship to you as do all other laws of nature. Through these laws of nature, you are a member of the outer world; and the outer world has a share in you that will reveal itself to you most clearly when you contemplate what the outer world does with your physical body after death. For life, the outer world gives you senses and an intellect, which make it impossible for you to see how the matter stands for your soul's experiencing beyond the boundary of death." To admit this can only lead to two possible results: either one suppresses all further investigation into the riddles of the soul and denies oneself the possibility of knowing anything in this realm, or one makes every effort to attain, through inner soul experience, what the outer world withholds. – These efforts can lead to making one's inner experiencing more powerful and energetic than it is in ordinary existence.

In ordinary life, a human being displays a certain degree of strength in his inner experiencing, in his life of feeling and thought. He might hold a thought in his mind only as often as there is an inner or outer reason to do so. However, any single thought can be taken from among the multitude of all other thoughts and, without any other reason, repeatedly thought through and inwardly experienced in a quite intensive way. One can repeatedly make such a thought the sole object of one's inner experiencing. And while doing this, one can hold at a distance all outer impressions and memories that tend to arise in one's soul. One can make such a full, exclusive devotion to thoughts, and also to feelings, into a regular inner practice. – If such inner experience is to lead to any truly meaningful results, it must be undertaken according to specific, tested laws. Such laws are recorded by the science of spiritual life. One can find a great number of them in my book *Knowledge of the Higher Worlds: How Is It Achieved?* – Through such an approach, one will succeed in intensifying one's forces of inner experiencing. Inner experience condenses, so to speak. One can recognize what happens as a result of this through the self-observations that will come about when this inner activity has been continued over a long enough period of time. In most cases, however, one needs much patience until convincing results come about. And whoever is not inclined to practice such patience for years will not achieve anything extraordinary.

It is only possible here to give an example of the results of such practice. The results are diverse in nature. What is described here is suitable for continuing the path of meditation whose beginning description has been given above.

A person may practice this inner intensification of soul life for a long time. He may experience nothing inwardly that would prompt him to think any differently about the world than he has been accustomed to so far. But then, one day, the following may happen. Naturally, what is described here will not happen to one person exactly as it does to another. Nevertheless, if one strives to form an inner picture of *one* such experience, then one will have enlightened oneself about the whole subject under consideration here.

A moment may arrive when the soul inwardly experiences itself quite differently than it usually does. In most cases, this will initially happen in such a way that the soul is enlivened from out of the state of sleep as if into a dream. Immediately, however, it becomes apparent that this experience cannot be compared to what are otherwise known to us as dreams. One is then completely transported out of the world of the senses and the intellect, and yet one experiences things as one does in normal existence when one is facing the outer world in the waking state. One feels compelled to picture, inwardly, what one is experiencing. To do so, one uses such concepts as one has at one's disposal in ordinary life. And yet one knows very well that one is experiencing something different from what those concepts usually relate to. One regards these concepts only as a means of expression that one uses for an experience one has not had before, and which one can also know to be impossible in ordinary existence. One feels as if surrounded on all sides by thunderstorms. One hears thunder and sees lightning. Yet one knows that one is in a room of a house. One feels oneself pervaded by a force of which one previously knew nothing. Then, one has the impression that one sees cracks in the surrounding walls. One is prompted to say to oneself, or to this or that person whom one believes to be standing nearby, "This is something serious. Lightning is going through the house; it is taking hold of me; I feel myself seized by it. It is dissolving me." – Once such a sequence of inner pictures has run its course, one's inner experience passes over to the ordinary state of mind. One finds oneself back in oneself with the memory of what was just experienced. If this memory is as lively and trustworthy as any other, then it also enables one to form a judgment concerning what was experienced. One then immediately knows that one has undergone something that could not be experienced either through the bodily senses or through the ordinary intellect. One will feel that a description such as that given above – whether for oneself or another – is no more than a means to express this experience. This expression is certainly a means of communicating about the matter; but it has nothing in common with it. One knows that for an experience of this kind one does not need any of one's senses. – Anyone who would speak here of a hidden activity of the senses or the brain knows nothing of the true form of such experiences. He forms his judgment only on the basis of the description that speaks of thunder, lightning, and cracks in the wall and, because of this, believes that the soul has experienced nothing but resonances of ordinary existence. He must regard what was experienced as a vision in the ordinary sense of the word. He cannot do otherwise than to think that this is so. He simply does not take into account that the one who describes such an experience, when using the words "thunder," "lightning," and "cracks in the wall," only considers them to be images for what he has experienced and does not mistake these images for the experience itself. It is right that it seems to him as if he actually perceived these images. But in such a case, he does not relate to the appearance of lightning as he normally would to a flash of lightning when seeing it with his eyes. The vision of lightning only forms for him something that is as though spread over the true experience. He sees something quite different through the lightning – something that cannot be experienced in the sensory outer world.

In order for a right judgment to come about, it is necessary for the soul that has had such an experience to be able to relate to the outer world in a completely healthy way once the experience is over. It must be able to correctly compare the special experience it has had with its experience of the ordinary outer world. Whoever is already inclined in ordinary life to let himself be swept away by all manner of sentimental rapture about things is ill-suited to form such a judgment. The healthier – one might even say, the more sober – a person's sense for reality, the better prepared he will be when forming a truthful and worthy assessment of such things. One can have confidence in one's own suprasensory experiences only if one can say, with regard to the everyday world, that one simply takes things and events as they are in a straightforward way.

If all these necessary conditions have been fulfilled, and one has good reason to assume that one has not fallen prey to an ordinary vision, then one knows that one has experienced something for which one did not make use of the body as a medium of observation. Instead, one has observed directly through the strengthened soul, without the support of the body. One has gained the inner picture of an experience *outside* the body.

It may be evident that, in this realm, the legitimate differences between reverie or illusion on one hand, and true observation conducted outside the body on the other, cannot be indicated in any other sense than they are in the realm of outer sense perception. It may happen that someone has a lively imagination when it comes to taste and, at the mere thought of lemonade, already feels as if he is actually drinking it. The difference between one experience and the other is indeed given by the whole context of life. And so it is, too, with experiences that one has outside the body. In order to arrive at completely convincing conceptions in this realm of experience, it is necessary to become familiar with it in a healthy way, to acquire the capacity to observe the contexts of what one experiences, and thus to correct one experience by way of another.

Through an experience of the kind described above, one has gained the possibility of observing what belongs to one's own self not merely by use of the senses and the intellect – that is, by use of the instruments of the body. One now not only knows something about the world other than what those instruments enable one to know; one also knows in a different way. This is especially important. A soul that passes through an inner transformation comes to recognize more and more that the pressing questions of existence cannot be solved within the sensory world because the senses and the intellect cannot penetrate deeply enough into the world. The souls that transform themselves in a way that enables them to experience outside the body do penetrate deeper. What can solve the riddles of the soul is to be found in the communications they are able to give of their experiences.

Now, an experience that takes place outside the body is of an entirely different nature than one within the body. This becomes clear through the assessment one can make of the experience described above when, once it is over, the normal wakeful state of soul has set in and the memory of the experience has emerged with sufficient vibrancy and clarity. The sensory body is felt by the soul to be separated from the rest of the world; the soul perceives it as belonging only to itself. This is not the case with what one experiences to be in oneself and with oneself when outside the body. There one feels oneself connected with all that one could call the outer world. One feels all that is in one's surroundings to be connected with oneself just as, in sensory life, one feels one's hand. There is no indifference on the part of the outer world toward the inner soul world. One feels oneself to be fully grown together and interwoven with everything that one can call the world. Its effects pass perceptibly through one's being. There is no sharp boundary between inner world and outer world. All of the surroundings belong to the observing soul, just as both hands of the body belong to the physical head. Nevertheless, one can say of a piece of that outer world that it belongs more to one's own self than does the rest of one's surroundings, just as one speaks of the head as an autonomous member relative to the hands or feet.

The soul calls a piece of the sense-perceptible outer world its body. A soul that is able to experience outside of this body can just as well consider a part of the non-sensory outer world as belonging to itself. If, therefore, the human being attains the ability to observe the realm that is accessible to him beyond the world of the senses, then he can say that a body belongs to him that is imperceptible to the senses. One may call this body the elemental or etheric body; but one should not mix into one's conception that fine substance which physics used to call "ether."

Just as mere reflection upon the relationship of the human being to the outer world of nature results in the conception of the physical body that corresponds to reality, so the soul's journeying into realms that can be perceived outside the sensory body leads to the recognition of an *elemental* or *etheric* body, or a body of formative forces.

# THIRD MEDITATION

## *The meditant attempts to form inner pictures concerning clairvoyant knowledge of the elemental world*

One experiences a world that remains unknown to sense perception and ordinary rational thinking when one perceives not through the sensory body, but rather outside it by means of the elemental body. If one wants to compare this world with something belonging to ordinary experience, then the world of memories, of inner pictures of recollection, presents itself as an apt comparison. Just as these rise up from the inner depths of the soul, so also do the suprasensory experiences of the elemental body. In the case of an inner picture of memory, however, the soul knows that it relates to an earlier experience within the sensory world. The suprasensory inner picture carries within it just as much of a relationship. Just as, by its nature, an inner picture of memory presents itself as something that one cannot describe as a mere product of fantasy, so too does the suprasensory inner picture. It wrests itself from the soul's experiencing, and yet right away reveals itself as an inner experience that relates to something outer. Through the inner picture of memory, something that was previously experienced becomes present in the soul. Through the suprasensory inner picture, something that exists sometime or somewhere in the suprasensory world becomes an inner soul experience. Thus, it becomes evident from the nature of the suprasensory inner pictures themselves that one can regard them as inwardly disclosed communications from a suprasensory world.

How far one goes with experiences in the suprasensory world in this way depends on how energetically one works on the strengthening of one's soul life. Whether one simply attains the concept that plants are not merely what one perceives within the confines of the sensory world, or whether one attains a similar concept with regard to the earth as a whole – both belong to the same realm of suprasensory experience. If someone who has acquired the capacity to perceive outside of his sensory body observes a plant, then he can perceive – in addition to what the senses show – a subtle form that permeates the whole plant. This form presents itself as a force-being; and he comes to regard this "force-being" as what forms the plant from out of the substances and forces of the sensory world and causes the circulation of its saps. He could then say, if he wishes to employ a useful if not entirely accurate expression: there is something in the plant that causes the saps to circulate, just as my own soul raises my arm. He sees the innermost essence of the plant, and he has to ascribe a certain autonomy to this innermost essence of the plant's being in relation to what the senses see of the plant. Furthermore, he must ascribe to this innermost essence an existence *preceding* that of the sensory plant. In this way, he comes to observe how a plant grows, wilts, produces seeds, and how out of these a new plant forms. The suprasensory force-form is especially powerful when the observation of a plant seed takes place. There, the sensory being is in a certain way unimposing; on the other hand, the suprasensory being is complex. It contains everything that collaborates in the forming and growing of the plant from out of the suprasensory world. – Suprasensory observation of the whole earth reveals a force-being that one can know with complete certainty to have existed prior to all that is sense-perceptible in what arose on and within the earth. By this means, one comes to experience the presence of the suprasensory forces that collaborated in the formation of the earth in the most distant past. What one experiences in this way may be called the etheric or elemental essential beings or bodies of plants and of the earth – just as one may call the body through which one perceives when outside the physical body one's own elemental or etheric body.

Even at an early stage of one's capacity for suprasensory observation, one will be led to ascribe to certain things and processes of the sensory world, in addition to their sensory characteristics, such elemental foundational beings. One will speak of an etheric body of the plant or of the earth. However, elemental beings observed in this way are certainly not the only ones that present themselves to suprasensory experience. One will say of the elemental body of a plant that it forms the substances and forces of the sensory world and by this means expresses itself in a sensory body. Yet one can also observe beings that lead an elemental existence without expressing themselves in a sensory body. Thus, for suprasensory observation, there are also purely elemental beings. One does not simply experience something that is added to the sensory world; one experiences a world within which the sensory world manifests itself, somewhat like pieces of ice floating in water. Whoever could see only the ice and not the water would find it possible to ascribe reality only to the ice and not to the water. Whoever limits himself only to what is revealed through the senses thereby denies the suprasensory world within which the sensory world is only one part – just as the pieces of ice floating in water are a part of the entire body of water.

One will now find that those individuals who are able to observe suprasensory realities employ expressions borrowed from sensory perceptions in order to describe what they spiritually see (*schauen*).[5] Thus, one will find that the etheric body of a being of the sensory world, or of a purely elemental being, is described as revealing itself as a self-contained, variously colored light-body. It is said that this body colorfully flashes up, glows, or shines, thereby communicating that this phenomenon of color or light is its way of expressing its life. But what the observer speaks of is actually completely invisible. In fact, he is well aware that the image of light or color has no more to do with what he perceives than, for example, the letters by which a fact is communicated have to do with the fact itself. But it is not the case that one has merely arbitrarily expressed something suprasensory in inner pictures that are based on sensation; on the contrary, in the course of that suprasensory observation, one has really had an experience that is similar to a sense impression. This is due to the fact that, during suprasensory experience, the release from the sensory body is not a complete one. The sensory body is indeed still present within the life of the elemental body and thus brings the suprasensory experience into a sensory form. The description that one gives of an elemental being will in fact be of a kind that resembles a visionary or fantastic combination of sensory impressions. When a description is given in this way, it is nevertheless a true account of what was experienced. For one has seen what one describes. The error that can potentially be made does not consist in depicting the image as such. The error arises only when one attributes reality to the image itself instead of seeking the reality in the corresponding fact that the image merely points to.

If a person who has never perceived colors – a person born blind – achieves the capacity described here, he will not portray elemental beings by saying, "They flash forth as color phenomena." In expressing himself, he will make use of those sensation-based inner pictures with which he is familiar. But for those who are able to physically see, a description that employs expressions such as "a color phenomenon flashes forth" is thoroughly appropriate. Through this, they can form a feeling for what the observer of the elemental world has seen spiritually. This holds true not only for what a clairvoyant (as we may call a person who can observe through his elemental body) communicates to those who are not clairvoyant, but also for how clairvoyants reach understanding among themselves. In the world of the senses, one simply lives in a sensory body, and this body clothes one's suprasensory observations in sensory forms. Therefore, within the confines of human earthly life, the expression of suprasensory observations through the sensory images engendered by them is indeed for now a useful mode of communication.

What is essential is that a person who receives such a communication has an experience in his soul that stands in a right relationship to the corresponding fact. Sensory images are used in these communications only so that something may be experienced through them. These sensory images cannot occur in the sensory world in the manner in which they here present themselves.

Precisely this is what is distinctive about them. And for this very reason, they call forth experiences that bear no relation to anything sensory.

At the beginning of clairvoyance, one will find it difficult to free oneself from bringing things to expression in sensory images. As one's ability increases, however, the need will arise to devise more intentional means of representation in order to communicate what was seen. From this, the necessity will arise to first clarify the particular signs that one is using. The more the culture of the time demands that suprasensory findings are made common knowledge, the more pronounced will be the need to communicate these findings through the means of expression taken from everyday life in the sensory world.

Suprasensory experiences may arise in such a way that at certain moments they simply occur. They then come over a person. And this person then has the opportunity to learn something about the suprasensory world through his own experience – in accordance with how he is more or less often graced, so to speak, by the suprasensory world shining into his ordinary soul life. However, a higher capacity is involved when it is a matter of intentionally bringing about clairvoyant observation from the ordinary soul life. The path to the achievement of this capacity usually becomes accessible through an energetically pursued inner strengthening of the soul life. Yet much also depends upon attaining a particular mood of soul. A calm, composed demeanor toward the suprasensory world is necessary – a demeanor that is just as far removed from a burning desire to attain the clearest and greatest possible amount of knowledge as it is from a personal lack of interest in the suprasensory world. Burning desire has the effect of spreading something like an invisible fog before one's body-free seeing. Lack of interest has the effect that, although suprasensory things actually do reveal themselves, they are simply not noticed. This lack of interest sometimes comes to expression in a quite special form. There are people who wish quite honestly to have experiences of clairvoyance, but they begin with a very definite inner picture of what these experiences should be like if they are to be recognized as genuine. And then, real experiences do come about; but they flit away without any interest having been brought to meet them, for they are not as one had imagined that they would be.

With clairvoyance that is intentionally brought about, a moment comes in the course of the soul's inner activity when one knows: "Now the soul is experiencing something it has not experienced before." The experience is nothing definite, but rather a general feeling that one is not facing the sensory outer world, that one is not in it – and yet, that one is also not in oneself as is the case in ordinary soul life. Inner and outer experience flow together, forming one basic feeling that was previously unknown to the soul – a feeling that the soul knows it could never experience if it were only living through the senses with the outer world, or if it were living in its ordinary feelings and inner pictures of memory. One then further senses that something is sliding into this soul state from a hitherto unknown world. But one is unable to come to an inner picture of this unknown something. One experiences, but one cannot inwardly picture. Rather, for the one having such an experience, there comes over him the feeling as if his physical-sensory body were presenting an obstacle to inwardly picturing what is forcing its way into the soul. However, if one continues one's inner soul-effort with perseverance, then after a while one will feel as if one is the overcomer of the resistance of one's own body. Until then, one's physically based intellectual apparatus has been suitable only for forming inner pictures connected with experiences in the sensory world. This apparatus is initially unable to raise to the level of an inner picture what wants to reveal itself from the suprasensory world. In order to be able to do so, it must first be worked upon. Just as a child is surrounded by the outer world and yet must first have its intellectual apparatus prepared through the experience of the outer world in order to form inner pictures about its surroundings, so too is a human being generally unable to inwardly picture the suprasensory world. The aspiring clairvoyant accomplishes with his inner picturing apparatus the same thing that happens within a child, only on a higher level. He lets his intensified thoughts work upon this apparatus, which is thereby gradually transformed. It then becomes capable of receiving the suprasensory world into the life of inner pictures. One feels how one works formatively, through one's soul activity, upon one's own body. At first, the body makes its presence felt in the form of a heavy counter-pressure against one's soul life. One feels it as a foreign body within one. Then one notices how one's body adjusts itself more and more to the experiencing of one's soul. Finally, one no longer feels the body but instead has before one the suprasensory world – just as one does not see the eye through which one perceives the world of color. The body must become imperceptible before the soul can see into the suprasensory world. If in this way one has managed to intentionally make one's soul clairvoyant, then as a rule one will always be able to call forth this state by concentrating oneself upon a thought that one can experience inwardly with particular intensity. As a consequence of giving oneself over to this thought, one will find that clairvoyance has been brought about. At first, one will not yet be in a position to see exactly those things that one wants to see. Suprasensory things and processes for which one is entirely unprepared, and which one in fact did not want to call forth, will play into one's soul. Nevertheless, when one continues the inner effort with perseverance, one will become able to direct one's spiritual gaze to things that one intends to perceive. Just as one can bring to memory a forgotten experience by calling forth in one's soul something similar to what has been forgotten, so, as a clairvoyant, one can start from an experience that one has reason to believe is related to what is sought. If one concentrates intensively upon the known experience, then after a shorter or longer period, what one intends to experience will often appear. In general, however, one should take into account that for the clairvoyant, calmly waiting for the favorable moments is of the greatest value. One should never want to force anything. If an experience one has striven for does not come about, it is good to resign oneself for the time being and try again to create that opportunity another time. The human knowledge-apparatus requires a calm ripening toward particular experiences. Whoever lacks the patience to wait for such a ripening will have incorrect or imprecise observations.

# FOURTH MEDITATION

## *The meditant attempts to form an inner picture of the "guardian of the threshold"*

Once the soul has achieved the capacity to observe something from outside the body, certain difficulties may arise in its feeling life. It may notice that it is compelled to assume an entirely different position in relation to itself than it was used to before. It had been facing the sensory world in such a way that it regarded that sensory world as an outer world and regarded the experiencing of the inner world as its own possession. The soul cannot relate to the suprasensory outer world in this way. As soon as the soul perceives that outer world, it flows, so to speak, together with it; it cannot conceive of itself as being separate from it in the way it does with regard to the sensory outer world. As a result, all that the soul, standing over against this suprasensory outer world, might call its own inner world takes on a certain peculiarity that is difficult at first to unite with the conception of inwardness. One can no longer say: "I think," or "I feel," or "I have my thoughts and form them." One must say: "Something thinks in me," or "Something causes feelings to light up in me," or "Something forms the thoughts so that they appear in a very specific way and signal their presence in consciousness."

Now this feeling can have something extraordinarily oppressive about it if the quality of suprasensory experience proves to be such that it produces the certainty that one is truly experiencing a reality, and not giving oneself over to a fantasy or illusion. Appearing in this way, this experience can show that the suprasensory outer world certainly wants to perceive itself through feeling, to think itself, but that it is hindered in achieving what it wants to bring about. At the same time, one receives the feeling that what here wants to enter the soul is the true reality, and that this true reality alone can elucidate what one has experienced as reality up until now. This feeling also assumes another form: the suprasensory reality manifests itself as something that infinitely outshines the value of what was previously known to the soul as reality. The reason there is something oppressive about this feeling is that one arrives at the thought that one *must* want to take the next step that one now has to take. Taking this step is contained in the very nature of what one has now become through one's inner experiencing. One would experience it as a denial of what one is – indeed, as an act of self-annihilation – if one were not to take this step. And yet, the feeling can also arise that one cannot take it; or, if one does take it – as far as it is possible to do so – it will still remain incomplete.

All of this then changes into the following inner picture: As the soul now is, a task lies before it that it cannot manage because, in its current state, it will not be received into the suprasensory outer world – for this world does not want to have the soul within it. Thus the soul comes to feel itself as being in contradiction to the suprasensory world and must say to itself: "You are not as you would have to be in order to merge with this world. But only this world can reveal to you the true reality, as well as how you yourself relate to this true reality; thus, you have cut yourself off from genuine observation of what is true." This feeling implies an experience that will become increasingly decisive for the whole worth of one's own soul. One feels oneself to be standing, with one's whole life, within an error. Yet this error differentiates itself from other errors. Those errors are thought, but this error is lived. An error that is thought may be undone by replacing the wrong thought with the right one. The lived error has become a part of the life of the soul itself; one *is* the error; one cannot simply ameliorate it; for one may think as one wants, but the error is there; it is a part of reality – indeed, of one's own reality. Such an experience has something devastating about it for one's own self. One feels one's inner life painfully repelled by everything that one longs for. This pain, which is felt at a certain stage of the soul's journeying, goes far beyond any pain that one can experience in the sensory world. Thus, it can also go far beyond all that one can manage as a result of one's own soul life up until now.

It can have a numbing effect. The soul stands before the anxious question: "Where shall I find the forces to bear what is being laid upon me here?" And it is within its own life that the soul must find these forces. They consist in something that may be called inner courage or inner fearlessness.

In order to come further in the soul's journeying, one must be led to the point where the forces for bearing one's experiences become accessible from out of one's inner life, calling forth inner courage and fearlessness in a way that one did not need for life within the sensory body. Such forces arise only from true self-knowledge. Basically, at this stage of development one first realizes how little one really knew about oneself before. One had surrendered to inner experiences without looking at them as one would a part of the outer world. However, it is through these steps – which have led to the capacity to experience outside the body – that one receives special means of attaining self-knowledge. One learns, so to speak, to observe oneself from a point of view that arises only when one is outside the sensory body. And the oppressive feeling mentioned is already the beginning of true self-knowledge. To experience oneself as living in error in one's relation to the outer world: that is what reveals one's soul being as it really is.

Now it lies in the nature of the human soul that it feels such enlightenment concerning itself to be painful. It is only when one feels this pain that one experiences how strong the entirely natural longing is to consider oneself, as a human being, valuable and significant just as one is. The fact that this is so may look ugly; one must freely face this ugliness of one's own self. The reason for not noticing this ugliness up until now is that one had never really penetrated one's own being with one's consciousness. It is only in such a moment that one notices how much one loves in oneself what one must now feel to be ugly. The power of self-love thus shows itself in its full magnitude. And, at the same time, it is shown how little inclined one is to cast off this self-love. As for those characteristics of soul that come into consideration in ordinary life and in one's relations with others, the difficulties they cause already prove great enough. But through true self-knowledge one comes to know, for example, that although one had thought one's feelings toward someone were friendly, one was actually harboring hidden jealousy, hatred, or the like in the depths of one's soul. One realizes that these feelings, which have not manifested themselves up until now, will most certainly force their way out one day. One perceives that it would be quite superficial to say to oneself: "Now that you have realized how matters stand with you, just go ahead and eradicate the jealousy and hatred." One soon discovers that such thoughts prove very weak when the urge to satisfy one's hatred or to express one's jealousy breaks forth from the soul as if with the power of an elemental force. Particular instances of self-knowledge like these arise in this or that person according to the individual soul's constitution. They come about upon the occurrence of experiences outside the body precisely because, in such moments, one's self-knowledge becomes a true self-knowledge – a self-knowledge that can no longer be clouded by the wish to see oneself in this or that way, in accord with how one would so love to be.

These particular instances of self-knowledge are painful; they are oppressive for the soul. But whoever wishes to acquire the capacity to experience outside the body cannot avoid them. For they inevitably do occur as a consequence of the very specific relation one must place oneself in with regard to one's own soul. Indeed, the strongest soul forces are required when it is a matter of an entirely universal human self-knowledge. One observes oneself from a viewpoint that lies outside of one's previous soul life. One says to oneself: "You have seen and judged the things and processes of the world according to your human nature and being. Now try to imagine for once that you could not see or judge things in that way. Then, you would not at all be who you are. You would have no inner experiences. You yourself would be a nothing." It is not only the person who stands in the midst of daily life, seldom forming conceptions about the world and life, who must speak to himself in this way. Every scientist and every philosopher must also do so. For philosophy, too, is only an observation and assessment of the world according to the qualities of human soul life. But such an assessment cannot flow together with the suprasensory outer world. It will be rejected by it. Consequently, everything that one has been so far is rejected with it. One looks back upon one's whole soul, upon one's 'I', as something one must discard if one wants to enter the suprasensory world. – Now, before the soul enters the suprasensory world, it can do nothing other than regard this 'I' as its actual being. It must see in the 'I' the human being's true essence. It must say to itself, "Through this 'I' of mine, I must form inner pictures about the world. I must not lose this 'I' of mine if I do not want to abandon myself as a being." The strongest instinct in the soul is always and everywhere to safeguard for itself the 'I', so that the soul does not lose the ground under its feet. Whereas the soul justifiably feels this way in ordinary life, it may no longer do so as soon as it enters the suprasensory outer world. Here, the soul must step across a threshold where it must leave behind not only this or that precious possession but also what it itself had been up to that point. It must be able to say to itself: "What you previously recognized as your strongest truth must now, on the other side of the threshold of the suprasensory world, be able to appear to you as the strongest error."

Faced with such a demand, the soul may shrink back. It may feel what it has to do as an abandoning of its own being, as a declaration of its own being's nothingness so intensely that it must basically admit to itself, when faced with this threshold, its own powerlessness to satisfy this requirement. This admission may take all possible forms. It may emerge quite instinctively; and to a person who acts and thinks in accordance with this admission, it may appear as something very different from what it actually is. He may, for example, feel a deep aversion toward all suprasensory truths. He may consider such truths to be daydreams or fantasies. But he does this only because in the depths of his soul – which are unknown to him – he harbors a secret dread toward these truths. He feels that he can live only with what is revealed by the senses and rational judgment. Therefore, he avoids approaching the threshold of the suprasensory world. He clothes that avoidance in the conviction, for instance, that what is supposed to lie beyond the threshold is untenable to reason and science. But the fact is simply that he loves reason and science, as he knows them, because they are bound to his 'I'. It is a matter of an entirely common human form of self-love. But this self-love cannot be taken along into the suprasensory world.

It may also happen that it does not remain a matter of this instinctive halting before the threshold. It may happen that the human being approaches the threshold quite consciously and then turns around because he feels dread in the face of what stands before him. It will then not be easy for him to blot out the ensuing effects upon his ordinary soul life of his having approached the threshold. These effects will consist in certain consequences that are spread throughout his whole soul being by the powerlessness which he felt.

What should happen consists in the person making himself capable, upon entering the suprasensory world, of casting aside what he perceives to be the strongest truth in ordinary life and of orienting himself in a different way in terms of how he perceives and judges things. But at the same time, he must be clear that, upon once again facing the world of the senses, he must resume his use of the way of perceiving and judging valid for that world. He must, therefore, learn not only to live in two worlds but also to live in each world in a quite different way. He must not allow his healthy power of judgment for ordinary life in the world of the senses and of the intellect to become impaired just because he is compelled to make use of a different way of forming judgments for a different world.

For the human nature and being, it is difficult to take up a position like this. One acquires the faculty for it only through the continued energetic and patient strengthening of one's soul life. Whoever undergoes the experience of the threshold will feel that it is a blessing for ordinary human soul life not to be led right up to this threshold. The feelings that arise in anyone who has done so are such that one cannot but attribute this blessing to a powerful being that protects one from the danger and terror of self-annihilation at the threshold. – Behind the outer world given in ordinary life, there lies another world. Before its threshold stands a stern guardian, who ensures that the human being experiences nothing of what exists as the laws of the suprasensory world. For all doubt, all uncertainty about that world is indeed easier to bear than the sight of what one must leave behind if one wishes to enter it.

The human being remains protected from the above experiences as long as he does not himself approach the threshold. The fact that he has received accounts of experiences from those who have stepped upon or crossed this threshold alters nothing about the fact that he is protected. On the contrary, such accounts can serve him well when he draws near to the threshold. It is the same in this case as it is in many others: if one is able, beforehand, to form an inner picture of a task, it will be better performed than if this were not the case. But what the traveler into the suprasensory world can gain in terms of self-knowledge is in no way diminished by such prior knowledge. Therefore, it does not correspond to the facts when clairvoyants, or those familiar with what clairvoyance is, assert that one should not speak of such things to those who are not themselves at the point of entering the suprasensory world. We live in an age in which human beings must become increasingly familiar with the nature of the suprasensory world if they are to be able, in their souls, to withstand life's challenges. The spreading of suprasensory knowledge, including knowledge of the guardian of the threshold, belongs to the tasks of the present and the immediate future.

## FIFTH MEDITATION

### *The meditant attempts to form an inner picture of the "astral body"*

When one experiences a suprasensory outer world through the elemental body, one is less closed off from this world than one is, in the sensory body, from one's physical surroundings. And yet, one has a relationship to this suprasensory outer world that may be expressed as follows: one stands in connection with certain substances of the elemental world that form a particular elemental body, just as one carries with one in the physical body the substances and forces of the physical outer world. One notices that this is the case when one wishes, outside one's sensory body, to orient oneself in the suprasensory world. It may happen that one is faced with some fact or being of the suprasensory world. It can be there; one can spiritually see it; but one does not know what it is. If one is strong enough, one may drive it away – but only through energetically concentrating on one's experience in the sensory world, and thereby transposing oneself back into that world. But one cannot remain in the suprasensory world and compare the fact or being that one saw with other facts or beings. This would be the only way of orienting oneself in relation to the meaning of what one has seen. Thus, seeing in the suprasensory world can be restricted in such a way that one perceives details but cannot freely move from one detail to another. One feels held fast by the particular detail.

Now one may seek the reason for this restriction. One will find it only if, through advancing in one's inner development in a way that still further strengthens one's soul life, one reaches the point at which, in a particular instance, the restriction is no longer there. But then one becomes aware that the reason why one could not move freely from one detail that was seen to another lies in one's own soul. One comes to recognize that seeing in the suprasensory world differs from perception in the sensory world in the following respect: In the latter, one can, for instance, see all that is visible if one's eyes are working properly. If one sees one thing, then one can see another thing through the same eyes. This is not the case in the suprasensory world. One may have developed the elemental body's suprasensory organ of observation in such a way that one is able to experience this or that suprasensory fact; in order to see yet another fact, this organ must first be developed further in a way that correlates specifically to this other fact. – Now as far such development is concerned, one has the feeling that it is as if this organ awakens for a particular part of the suprasensory world. One feels, in relationship to the suprasensory world, as if the elemental body were in a kind of sleep state – as if it had first to be woken up for each particular detail. One can actually speak of a sleeping and waking in the elemental world. However, for this world sleeping and waking are not alternating states as they are within life in the sensory world. Rather, both states are simultaneously present in the human being. As long as one has not acquired the capacity to experience something through the elemental body, the elemental body sleeps. One always has this body with one, but it is asleep. With the strengthening of soul life, the awakening process begins, but at first only for a part of this body. One lives more and more into the elemental world by awakening more and more of one's own elemental being.

In the elemental world itself, there is nothing that can help the soul in this awakening. Regardless of how much one might be able to spiritually see already, nothing of what one has already seen will contribute to the seeing of anything else. Free mobility in the suprasensory world cannot be achieved by the soul through anything that could be found in the elemental environment. The continuing of one's exercises in soul-strengthening is what will allow one to increasingly achieve this mobility in certain realms. Through all of this, one will become aware of something in oneself that does not belong to the elemental world, but which one discovers in oneself through experiencing the elemental world. One finds oneself as a unique being in the suprasensory world: a being that appears to oneself as a ruler of one's elemental body – as the master of this body, the one who gradually awakens it into a suprasensory consciousness.

Once one has achieved this, an immense feeling of loneliness overcomes the soul. One sees oneself in a world that is elemental on all sides; one sees only oneself within the endless elemental expanses, as a being that cannot find others of its own kind anywhere. – It should not be claimed that *every* path of development toward clairvoyance will lead to this immense loneliness; yet anyone who consciously acquires this soul-strengthening by his own efforts will reach this point. And whoever follows a teacher who guides him from step to step in order to help him advance in his development will inevitably realize – and he may do so late, but he will certainly do so one day – that his teacher has left him to himself. At first, he will find that he has been abandoned by his teacher and given over to loneliness in the elemental world. Only retrospectively will he recognize that the teacher has dealt with him wisely: that the teacher had to consign him to his own resources when the necessity for such self-reliance arose.

Like an outcast who has been exiled into the elemental world – this is how the human being feels himself at this stage of the soul's journeying. But having reached this point, he can progress still further if he has accrued enough soul force through his inner exercises. He can begin to see the emergence – not in the elemental world, but in himself – of a world that is not one and the same as the sensory world or the elemental world. For such a person, a second suprasensory world is now added to the first suprasensory world. This second suprasensory world is, to begin with, an entirely inner world. One feels that one carries it within oneself and is alone with it. If one wants to compare this condition with something in the sensory world, the following case immediately suggests itself. Imagine that someone has seen all of his beloved relatives die away and now carries in his soul only memories of them. For him, it is as if they live on only as his thoughts. – One is in the second suprasensory world in the same way. One carries this world within oneself, but one knows that one is closed off from its reality. It is only that the element of this reality that lives in the soul has an entirely different reality than do mere inner pictures of memory in the sensory world. Within one's own soul, this suprasensory world leads an independent existence. All of what is there wants to leave the soul, wants to go join with something else. Thus one feels a world in oneself, but in such a way that this world does not want to stay in the soul. This gives rise to a feeling as if every detail of that world could make one burst. One can reach the point where these details free themselves and, tearing through something like a soul sheath, escape the soul. Then, one may feel the poorer for all that has thus torn itself away from the soul. –

One now comes to recognize that any suprasensory soul-content that one can love – and love solely for its own sake, not just because it is in one's own soul – behaves in a certain way. What one can love devotedly in this way does not tear itself from the soul; it will indeed force itself out of the soul, but in a certain sense it will take the soul with it. It will lead the soul to where it lives in its reality. A kind of union with the real being takes place, whereas previously one carried only something like an afterimage of this being within one. The love characterized here must, however, be one that is experienced in the suprasensory world. In the sensory world, one can only prepare oneself for such a love. And one does indeed prepare oneself when one makes strong one's capacity for love in the sensory world. The stronger the love one is capable of in the sensory world, the more of that capacity to love will remain with the soul for the suprasensory world. As for the particulars of the suprasensory world, this means, for example, that one cannot reach those real suprasensory beings connected with the plants of the sensory world if one does not love plants in the sensory world. And yet, with regard to such things, a misconception may easily occur. It can happen that, in the sensory world, a person quite lovelessly passes the plant world by; yet, within his soul, a hidden, unconscious inclination toward the plant world may be present. Then, this love can awaken when he enters the suprasensory world.

Just as uniting with beings of the suprasensory world can depend on love, so can such uniting also depend on other qualities of the soul, such as the respect or veneration that a soul can feel within the suprasensory world for a being once it feels that being's afterimage arising within it. However, these qualities are always ones that can be counted among the inner soul-qualities. – Thus, one will come to know those beings of the suprasensory world to which the soul itself opens the way through such qualities. A secure path to orientation in the suprasensory world opens up by the fact that, through the way one relates to the afterimages of these beings, one frees one's access to them. In the sensory world, one loves a being after one has come to know it; in the second suprasensory world, one can love the image before encountering the corresponding reality, because the image manifests itself before that encounter.

What the soul comes to know within itself in this way is not the elemental body. For in relation to this body, the soul rather stands as its awakener. Instead, what one comes to know is a being that is present within one's soul: a being that one experiences in the same way as one would experience oneself during sleep if one were not unconscious, but rather felt oneself to be conscious outside of one's physical body – and then, upon awakening, felt oneself to be the awakener. Thus the soul learns to know a being that is present within the soul itself, and which constitutes a third entity in addition to the physical and elemental bodies. This being may be called the *astral body*, and with these words is meant, for the moment, nothing more than what experiences itself within the soul's being in the way described.

## SIXTH MEDITATION

### *The meditant attempts to form an inner picture of the "I-body" or "thought-body"*

One has a stronger feeling of being outside the sensory body during experience within the astral body than during experience within the elemental body. In the latter, one feels oneself to be outside the realm in which the sensory body exists, and yet one still continues to feel its presence. In the astral body, however, one feels the sensory body itself as something outer. Crossing over into the elemental body, one experiences something like an expansion of one's own being. When immersing oneself in the astral body, on the other hand, one experiences a kind of "leaping over into" another being. And one feels a spiritual world of beings working into this being. One feels oneself to be in one way or another connected with, or related to, these beings. And gradually, one learns to perceive how these beings themselves interrelate. For human consciousness, the world expands toward the spirit. The human being sees spiritual beings who, for example, bring it about that the successive epochs in the evolution of humanity are, in their character, truly determined by beings. These beings are the time spirits or primal forces. One may also come to know other beings whose soul-existence unfolds in such a way that their thoughts are simultaneously the active forces of nature. One is thus led to acknowledge that it is only for sensory perception that the forces of nature appear to be as sensory perception believes them to be. In fact, one is led to acknowledge that wherever a force of nature is active, it is actually the expression of a being's thought – just as, in the movement of a hand, it is the human soul that expresses itself. – Now all this certainly does not mean that on the basis of some kind of theory, one attaches to the processes of nature the notion of beings standing behind these processes. Rather, a person who experiences himself in the astral body enters into just as concrete and non-conceptual a relationship with those beings as one has in the sensory world with other individual human beings. – Among the beings whose realm one enters in this way, a graduated order may be distinguished, and one can thus speak of a world of higher hierarchies. Those beings whose thoughts reveal themselves to sensory perception as the forces of nature may be called the spirits of form.

Experience in this second suprasensory world brings about the condition that one feels one's own being, as it is in the sense world, to be something "outer" in the same way that, in sensory existence, one looks upon a plant as an outer being. – One will feel this experience of "being outside of" what in ordinary life one *must* feel to be the whole scope of one's own being as extremely painful, as long as another experience is not added. With energetic, inner soul work that leads to the proper concentration and strengthening of the soul life, precisely this pain need not arise to any acute degree. For a slow, gradual entry into this other experience may occur during the process of living into the astral body.

This other experience will consist in the fact that one is able to experience everything that previously was in and of one's own soul as a kind of memory, so that one now stands in the same relation to one's own former 'I' as one does to one's memories in the sensory world. Only through such an experience does one gain complete consciousness of the fact that one truly lives with one's own being in a world quite different from the sensory world. From now on, one possesses knowledge of the fact that one's former 'I' is something one only carries with one, and that this former 'I' is something different from what one *is*. One can now face one's own self. One receives an inner picture of what is now facing one's own soul and of which the soul previously said: "I myself am that." Now the soul no longer says, "I myself am that," but, "That is something I carry with me." Just as in ordinary life the 'I' feels independent with respect to its memories, so now the newly acquired 'I' feels independent in relation to the earlier 'I'. It feels that it belongs to the world of purely spiritual beings. And from the way this experience presents itself – and indeed from this and not from a theory – one recognizes what one previously regarded as one's 'I'-being itself. It now appears as a fabric of inner pictures of memory produced by the sensory, elemental, and astral bodies in the same way as a mirror produces mirror images. As little as a person considers himself to be *one* with his mirror image – just as little does a soul experiencing itself in the spiritual world consider itself to be *one* with what it experiences of itself in the sensory world. Naturally, the comparison with the mirror image can be taken only as a comparison. After all, the mirror image ceases when one changes one's position in relation to the mirror. The fabric that is woven, as it were, from inner pictures of memory, and that represents what one considers to be one's own being as long as one is in the sensory world, has much greater autonomy than a mirror image. In its own way, it is a being in its own right. Yet, compared to true soul-existence, it is rather like an image of its own being. The soul in its true existence feels that it needs this image for the purpose of self-revelation. It knows that it is itself something different, but it also knows that it would never have reached the point of truly knowing anything about itself if it had not first comprehended its own likeness in that world which – after its ascent into the spiritual world – became an outer world for it.

The fabric of inner pictures of memory, which, from now on, one looks upon as one's earlier 'I', may be called the "*I-body*" or "*thought-body*." In this context, however, the word "body" must be understood in a broader sense than one is accustomed to. "Body" here means all that one experiences about oneself of which one does not say, "I *am* that," but of which one says, "I *have* that with me." It is only when clairvoyant consciousness has reached the point of looking upon what it had previously called its own self in the same way as it would look upon a sum of inner pictures of memory that it can have an experience of what, in the real sense, is concealed behind the phenomenon of death. For it has now come to the point of touching the living reality of a truly existing world in which it feels itself as a being that is able to retain, as in memory, what is experienced in sensory existence. What has been experienced in sensory life, in order to continue to live out its existence, needs a being that can hold fast to it just as the inner pictures of memory are held fast by the ordinary 'I' in sensory life. Suprasensory insight reveals that the human being has an existence in the world of spiritual beings, and that it is this human being himself who preserves his sensory existence like a memory within his own being. Therefore, to the question, "What might become of all that I am now when I die?" clairvoyant research replies, "You will be what you preserve of yourself by virtue of your existence as a spirit being among other spirit beings."

One comes to know the nature of these spirit beings, and within these, one's own nature. This knowledge is immediate experience. Through this experience one knows that spirit beings, and with these also one's own soul, have an existence for which sensory being is a passing manifestation. – To ordinary consciousness, it becomes evident – in the way shown in the first meditation – that the body belongs to a world whose true share in this body becomes manifest in its dissolution after death. Clairvoyant observation, on the contrary, makes it evident that the human 'I'-being belongs to a world to which it is bound by bonds very different from those that bind the body to the laws of nature. The bonds that bind the 'I'-being with the spiritual beings of the suprasensory world are not touched in their innermost essence by birth and death. These bonds manifest themselves in the sensory life of the body only in a special way. What appears in this life is the expression of relations that are of a suprasensory kind. Since a human being is a suprasensory being and appears as such to suprasensory observation, the relation in the suprasensory world between one human soul and another is unaffected by death. Thus, the anxious question imposing itself upon the soul in its ordinary state of consciousness, however primitively formulated it might be – "After death, will I see those I know and am connected to in earthly life?" – must be answered by authentic research with a clear "Yes."

All that has been said here about the experiencing of the soul being as a spiritual reality within the world of other spirit beings, may be seen spiritually by means of what has often been referred to here as the strengthening of one's soul life. Yet one can additionally foster this experience by cultivating in oneself particular feelings. – In ordinary experience in the sensory world, one stands in relation to what one perceives as one's destiny in such a way that one responds to one thing with feelings of sympathy and to another with feelings of antipathy. Self-reflection, which must be completely objective and impartial with regard to oneself, would have to admit that of all sympathies and antipathies a human being is able to feel, these [destiny-related ones] in particular are among the strongest. A simple reflection of the kind which says that everything that happens in life is in some way necessary, that one must bear one's destiny, may certainly achieve much for a composed attitude toward life. But in order to achieve something that contributes to a grasp of the true being of man, still more is needed. The reflection just described serves the life of the soul well; yet one will often notice that the sympathies and antipathies one casts aside have disappeared only from one's immediate consciousness. They have withdrawn into the depths of human nature and continue to live there as a soul mood, or perhaps as a feeling of weariness or some other bodily feeling. True equanimity with regard to destiny will only be attained if one proceeds in the same way in this field as one does when one repeatedly and intensively devotes oneself to thoughts or feelings that are conducive to soul-strengthening in general. Reflection alone – taking one no further than intellectual insight – is not sufficient. One must repeatedly, during certain periods of time, retain this reflection in one's soul and simultaneously ward off all sensory experiences and all other memories from one's life. Through such an exercise, one will achieve a certain basic mood of soul toward one's own life destiny. One can thoroughly drive out all antipathies and sympathies in this field so that, finally, one will be able to bear the sight of any event that could conceivably befall a person in the same detached way as a mere onlooker would watch a stream of water falling over a cliff and breaking upon the ground. This is not to say that as a result one should face one's destiny without feeling. Whoever comes to look with indifference upon everything that happens to him is certainly not on a fruitful path. But even with regard to what does not touch one's soul in the form of destiny, one actually does not face the outer world without participation. One sees what plays out before one's eyes with joy or with aversion. One who strives to attain suprasensory knowledge should not aspire to non-participation in life, but rather to a transformation of the share that the 'I' has in all that touches it as destiny. It is quite possible that through this transformation, the liveliness of one's feeling life is even intensified, not weakened. In ordinary life, tears would well up in one's eyes many a time over what might affect one's own soul in the way of destiny. However, one can work through to a view of life that causes one to cultivate the same clear feeling toward one's own misfortune as one does when a similar misfortune affects another person. It is easier to achieve this kind of experience with regard to blows of fate than, for example, with regard to one's capacities. For it is indeed not so easy to think that one will be able to rejoice in another's ability with the same joy that one would feel if one were to possess it oneself. When self-observation seeks to penetrate into the deepest foundations of the soul, quite a lot of selfish joy may be discovered with regard to everything one is able to do. An intense and repeated (meditative) "living together with" the thought that, in many ways, it is of no consequence for the course of human life whether it is one oneself who is able to do something or whether it is others who are able to, can bring one a long way toward genuine equanimity regarding what one feels as one's innermost destiny. When employed in the right way, such thought-invigorated strengthening of soul life *never* leads to a mere blunting of the feeling for one's own capacities. Rather, one transforms this feeling. One senses the necessity of adjusting one's actions to the capacities one really has.

And with this, the direction taken by such a thought-invigorated strengthening of soul life is already indicated. One learns to recognize within oneself something that appears to one as a second being within one's own soul. It manifests itself especially clearly when one connects to it thoughts that show how, in ordinary life, one brings about this or that event in one's destiny. One can indeed perceive: "This or that event would not have happened to you if you yourself had not behaved in a certain way at an earlier time." What happens to a person today is often simply a result of what he did yesterday. With the aim of leading one's soul experience further than it is at a certain point in time, one may now undertake a retrospective view into one's past soul experiences. In doing so, one can seek out all that shows how one had prepared one's own later destiny events. In such a review of life, one can try to reach back to the moment in which, as a child, one's consciousness awoke in such a way that enabled it to remember, later in life, what it had experienced. If, to this review, one applies the soul mood of eliminating all of the common selfish sympathies and antipathies toward the events of destiny, then, when one reaches in memory this very moment in one's childhood, one will be able to say to oneself: "At that moment, it first became possible for you to feel yourself within yourself and to work consciously upon your soul life. And yet, your 'I' was also there before. It did not knowingly work within you, but it did bring you your capacity for knowledge as well as all that you now know." What cannot be understood through intellectual consideration is actually brought about by an attitude toward one's personal destiny as it has been described above. One learns to face the incidents of destiny, but with composure. One objectively watches them approach, but one spiritually sees oneself in the being that brings these incidents toward one. And when one spiritually sees oneself in this way, then the conditions of one's own destiny – which are already given at birth – prove to be related to one's own self. Then one can bring oneself to the point of saying to oneself: "Just as you have worked upon yourself in the time following the awakening of your consciousness, so you were already working upon yourself before your present consciousness awoke." Such a working through to a higher 'I'-being within the ordinary 'I' not only enables one to say to oneself, "It is my thinking that prompts me to theoretically conceive of such a higher 'I'" – but rather, it enables one to feel the living being of the 'I' as a reality and as a power that lives within one's own self, and to sense the ordinary 'I' to be a creation, within one's own self, of this other 'I'. To feel this means to really begin to spiritually see the soul as a spirit being. And if it leads to nothing, that is only because one has allowed oneself to stop at the beginning. This beginning may consist in a barely noticeable dim feeling. It may remain so for a long time. But if one further pursues with strength and force what led to this beginning, one will in the end come to spiritually see the soul as a spirit being. Whoever has achieved this spiritual seeing will find it quite understandable when someone who has gained no experience in this realm says that whoever believes himself to have seen such things has only brought himself, through psychological practices, to a mere fantasy – an autosuggestion – of the "higher I." But one who is capable of such seeing knows that objections of this kind arise only from lack of experience. Whoever earnestly works through all that has been described here will also acquire the capacity to discern his fantasy from reality. The inner experiences and pursuits that prove necessary in the course of such a soul-journeying, if it is to be undergone in the right way, will lead one to apply the strictest vigilance toward oneself in questions of fantasy and reality. When one purposefully strives to experience oneself as a spirit being in one's higher 'I', one will perceive that the central experience consists in what was characterized at the beginning of this meditation, and will recognize what was described in the second part as a support in one's soul-journeying.

# SEVENTH MEDITATION

## *The meditant attempts to form inner pictures concerning the nature of experience in suprasensory worlds*

The experiences that have proven necessary for the soul that intends to penetrate into the suprasensory worlds may appear daunting to some people. A person who feels daunted may well say to himself, "I don't know what would happen to me if I were to venture into these processes, nor how I would bear them." Under the influence of feelings of this kind, the thought easily arises that it is better not to interfere artificially in the soul's course of development, but instead to calmly surrender to guidance that remains unconscious and wait to see what this might bring for one's inner life in the future. A thought of this kind, however, will always be repressed by one who is able to bring another thought fully to life within himself: namely, that it is in one's very nature as a human being to advance oneself, and that it would mean an abandoning of one's duty if one were not to actively concern oneself with the forces that await their unfolding in the soul, instead leaving them to wither. Forces of self-development exist in every human soul. And there isn't a single soul that would not heed the call to unfold them if in some way it could experience something of these forces and their significance.

Moreover, no one would allow himself to be deterred from the ascent into higher worlds unless he were to adopt, in advance, an incorrect attitude toward the processes he will have to undergo. These processes are such as have been presented in the previous meditations. And if one intends to bring them to expression in words – which, of course, can be taken only from ordinary human life – then it is only by presenting them in this way that they can be correctly expressed. For experiences on the path of suprasensory knowledge stand in such a relation to the human soul that they are absolutely the same as what an increased feeling of loneliness, or the feeling that one is floating above a bottomless abyss, or any other feeling of this kind can mean to the human soul. In the course of experiencing such feelings, the forces needed for the path of knowledge will bring themselves forth. They are the seeds for the fruits of suprasensory knowledge. In a certain way, all of these experiences carry something deeply hidden within them. And when these experiences are lived through, what is hidden is brought to its greatest tension; something bursts through the feeling of loneliness – which is like a sheath surrounding this "something" – and surges forth into soul life as a means of knowledge.

But one must always take into consideration that when the right path is pursued, behind every such experience another immediately arises. If the first experience is there, then the other cannot fail to appear. What one has to bear will immediately be accompanied by the power to really bear it if only one contemplates calmly and takes the time to notice what is seeking to reveal itself in one's soul. If something painful happens, and at the same time a feeling of certainty lives in the soul that there exist forces that can make the pain bearable and with which one can unite oneself, then one will reach the point of relating to such experiences – which would be unbearable if they were to occur in the course of ordinary life – as if one were the observer of oneself in all that one experiences. For this reason, those who are on the path of suprasensory knowledge do inwardly live through the ebb and flow of many waves of feeling and yet show perfect equanimity in their sensory lives. – For it is indeed quite possible that experiences taking place in the inner world will also affect the mood of one's outer life in the sensory world in such a way that, for a time, one may not be able to come to terms with life and oneself as one had before entering upon the path of knowledge. One is then obliged to draw from what one has already achieved inwardly in order to find the forces that will enable one to cope again. And no situation could arise on the rightly pursued path of knowledge in which this is not possible.

The best path of knowledge will always be one that, with the power of thought or feeling, leads to the suprasensory world through the strengthening or condensing of one's soul life by means of inner contemplation. The point is not to experience the thought or feeling in the way we do in order to orient ourselves within the sensory world, but rather that one lives intensively *with* and *in* the thought or feeling, and that one concentrates all of one's soul forces into it. During the time of inner contemplation, it alone should wholly fill one's consciousness. For example, one may think of a thought that has brought a sense of conviction to the soul. For the moment, one leaves aside this thought's weight of conviction and simply lives with the thought so that one becomes completely *one* with it. It is not necessary for this thought to relate to the things of the higher world order, although a thought that does so will be useful to a heightened degree. A thought that reflects an ordinary experience can also be used for inner contemplation. As for feelings, especially fruitful are those that reflect some resolution to perform a deed of love – feelings that one may then enkindle within oneself into the most intense experience of human warmth and sincerity. When dealing predominantly with knowledge, however, symbolic inner pictures are especially effective: inner pictures that one may have acquired in life, or to which one devotes oneself upon the advice of those knowledgeable in this area – those who know how fruitful these means are on account of what has come about for them through their application.

Through such contemplation – which must become a life habit, indeed a condition of life, just as breathing is a condition for the life of the body – one gathers together the forces of the soul and, in gathering, strengthens them. One must only succeed, during those periods of inner contemplation, in completely controlling oneself in such a way that neither outer sensory impressions nor any memories of them are able to tinge one's soul life. Likewise, all those memories of what one has experienced in ordinary life, of what gave the soul joy or pain, must be silent so that the soul is completely and solely devoted to *what one oneself has determined.* The forces for suprasensory knowledge grow in the right way *only* from what one has achieved through such periods of inner contemplation, the content and form of which one has oneself produced by mobilizing the power of one's own soul. It does not matter from where one has acquired the content of the contemplation. One may have received it from a person knowledgeable in this realm, or from spiritual-scientific literature. One must only be sure to make this content one's own inner experience, rather than allowing oneself to be prompted to undertake a contemplation only through what comes from one's own soul or through what one personally regards as the best content for a contemplation. The latter has very little force, because the soul feels related to it from the outset and so does not need to exert the necessary effort toward becoming one with it. *It is in these efforts*, and not in being united with the content of the contemplation as such, that the effective means for the development of suprasensory forces of knowledge lie.

It is also possible to achieve suprasensory seeing in other ways. It can happen that individuals, by virtue of their whole predisposition, come to inner deepening, to fervent experiencing. Suprasensory forces of knowledge can thereby be released within their souls. Such forces can often arise suddenly in souls that may seem not at all predestined to have experiences of this kind. Suprasensory soul life may emerge in the greatest variety of ways. Yet only by following the path of knowledge described here can an experience of the suprasensory come about that is able to regulate itself in the same way that one is able to regulate oneself in one's ordinary sensory existence. Every other form in which the suprasensory world can break into the soul's experiences leads to a situation in which these experiences set in as if by compulsion and in which one comes under their control. It can also lead to a situation in which one lays oneself open to every kind of deception regarding the value or true significance of these experiences within the actual suprasensory world.

One must indeed bear in mind that the soul transforms on the path of suprasensory knowledge. It may be the case that as far as sensory life is concerned, one has no disposition at all to be taken in by illusions and deceptions. And yet, as soon as one enters the suprasensory world, one may naively succumb to deceptions and illusions in the most credulous manner. It may also happen that in sensory existence one has a good and healthy sense for truth that tells one: you should not believe this or that about some fact or event simply because it satisfies your sense of self (*Selbstsinn*). And yet, even though this may be the case, such a soul can be led to spiritually see in the suprasensory world what is in keeping with that sense of self. Consider how this sense of self takes an active part in what one spiritually sees. One sees that which this sense of self directs itself toward according to its inclinations. One does not realize that it is just this sense of self that directs one's spiritual gaze. And it is thus entirely understandable that one takes what one sees for the truth. The only possible safeguard against this is to better and better prepare oneself – by means of proper self-reflection and an energetic will toward self-knowledge on the path of suprasensory knowledge – to notice how much sense of self is present in one's soul and to notice when it is speaking. One will be able to gradually break away from being led by the sense of self only if, in one's inner contemplation, one unsparingly and energetically faces the possibility that one's own soul may here or there succumb to the sense of self.

It belongs to the true, unhindered mobility of the soul in the higher worlds that this soul acquires a direct experience of how differently certain soul qualities relate to the spiritual world than they do to the sensory world. This is especially evident when one considers the moral qualities of the soul. Within the scope of sensory existence, a distinction is made between natural laws and moral laws. If one wishes to explain the course of natural processes, one cannot draw upon moral conceptions. One explains a poisonous plant by means of natural laws and does not judge it morally because it is poisonous. One will even be clear about the fact that with regard to the animal world, one can at best speak only of echoes of morality; but a moral judgment in the genuine sense would only distort what truly comes into consideration there. It is only in the context of human life that moral judgment with regard to the *value* of existence begins to have meaning at all. For human beings – once one is able to judge oneself in an unbiased way – this capacity for moral judgment is the authority that one will always refer to in assessing one's own value. Upon closer consideration of sensory existence, however, it would never occur to anyone to view natural laws as being equal or even similar to moral laws.

As soon as one enters the higher worlds, the situation is different. The more spiritual the worlds are that one enters, the more do moral laws and what one may call the "natural" laws of those worlds coincide. When in sensory existence we say that an evil deed burns in someone's soul, we know we are speaking figuratively. We know that burning in the natural world is something quite different. A similar distinction does not exist in the suprasensory worlds. There, hatred and envy are forces that act in such a way that their effects may also be referred to as the natural processes of these worlds. There, hatred or envy cause the being that is hated or envied to have a devouring or extinguishing effect on the being that hates or envies, so that destructive forces are formed which are damaging to that spiritual being. Love works in the spiritual world in such a way that one may speak of its effect as radiant warmth that is generative and supportive. – This may already be observed in the human elemental body. In the sensory world, the act of a hand that commits an immoral deed must be explained by the same natural law that explains a hand that serves a moral purpose. Certain elemental parts of the human being, however, remain undeveloped when the corresponding moral feelings do not exist. And, just as in sensory existence one explains natural processes through natural laws, so too one must see the reason for the imperfect development of elemental organs in imperfect moral qualities. But one should never conclude from the imperfect development of a sensory organ that the corresponding part of the elemental body is also imperfectly developed. One must always bear in mind that quite different kinds of laws are valid in different worlds. A person may have an imperfectly developed physical organ, while it may be the case that the corresponding elemental organ is not only "perfect" to a normal degree but, in fact, perfect to the same degree to which the physical organ is imperfect.

The difference between the suprasensory and the sensory worlds is also significant with regard to everything having to do with one's conceptions of "beauty" and "ugliness." The way in which these concepts are used in the sensory world loses all meaning as soon as one enters the suprasensory worlds. There, a being can be said to be "beautiful" – taking into account the exact meaning of the word in sensory existence – only if it is able to reveal all of what it experiences *within itself* to the other beings of its world so that these other beings may partake in the entirety of its experience. The capacity to completely reveal oneself and everything that lives within one without having to conceal anything within oneself could be called "beautiful" in the higher worlds. There, this concept of beauty coincides perfectly with what might be called wholehearted sincerity, the honest acting out of what one carries within oneself. A being might be called "ugly" that does not want to reveal its inner content through its outer appearance and that holds back its own experience in itself, concealing certain characteristics from other beings. Such a being withdraws from its spiritual surroundings. This concept of ugliness coincides with an insincere manner of revealing oneself. Lying and being ugly are one and the same *reality* in the spiritual world; consequently, a being that behaves in an ugly way is a lying being.

Also, everything that one recognizes as desires or wishes in the sensory world has a quite different meaning in the spiritual world. Such desires, which arise from the inner nature of the human soul in the sensory world, do not exist in the spiritual world. What one may call desires in the spiritual world are kindled by what is spiritually seen outside the being itself. A being that must feel itself lacking in a certain quality which, according to its nature, it ought to have, sees another being that has this quality. Then it can do nothing but have this other being continually before it. Just as the eye naturally sees what is visible in the sensory world, so in the suprasensory world a being is always guided by the lack of a quality into the vicinity of a being that is perfect in that regard. Consequently, the being burdened by the defect will feel the desire to correct this defect. This experience is of a quite different kind compared to the experience of desire in the sensory world. – Free will, however, is not affected by such relationships in the spiritual world. A being may fight against what the sight of something arouses within it. In this way, it will gradually succeed in getting farther away from the exemplary being. However, for such a being that defends itself against its ideal, the consequence is that this being thereby transposes itself into worlds in which it will find conditions of existence worse than those it had been given in the world for which it was actually predestined.

All this shows the human soul that its world of inner pictures must be transformed when it enters into the suprasensory worlds. In order to describe the suprasensory world correctly, one's concepts must be changed, expanded, or merged with others. – For this reason, there is always something inadequate about descriptions of the suprasensory world that use concepts coined for the sensory world without any further modification. – One may reflect that it is a product of true human feeling when concepts that only attain their full meaning in the suprasensory world are used in the sensory world more or less symbolically, but also as truly characterizing the matter in question. This is why someone may really feel what is of a lying nature to be ugly. Nevertheless, compared to the reality of this concept in the suprasensory world, its verbal use in sensory existence is only an echo that comes about because all worlds are related to one another and these relationships are dimly felt and unconsciously thought in sensory existence. Yet one must bear in mind that, in sensory existence, something of a lying nature that one *feels* to be ugly need not be ugly in its outer appearance. One would be confusing one's conceptions entirely if one sought to explain something ugly in sensory life as the product of the quality of lying. But in the suprasensory world, the situation is such that anything of a lying nature, when it is seen truly, brings itself to manifestation as something ugly. – Here again, however, deceptions come into consideration against which one must guard oneself. The soul may meet in the suprasensory world a being that one would rightly describe as evil, but which manifests itself in an image that one would call "beautiful" if one were to apply the concept of "beauty" brought along from sensory existence. In this case, one will see the being correctly only if one can penetrate to its inner foundation. One will then experience how the "beautiful" manifestation is only a mask that does not correspond to the being; and what one was ready to feel as "beautiful" based on conceptions drawn from sensory existence, one will then address, with particular intensity, as ugliness. In the very moment one succeeds in this, the "evil" being is no longer in a position to project the illusion of "beauty." To such an observer, the being must reveal itself in its true form, which can only be an incomplete expression of what it is in its inner nature. Such phenomena of the suprasensory world demonstrate particularly vividly how human conceptions must change upon entry into the suprasensory world.

## EIGHTH MEDITATION

*The meditant attempts to form an inner picture of the spiritual seeing of the human being's repeated earthly lives*

It is not actually justified to speak of dangers in the soul's journeying into suprasensory worlds as long as this journeying is undertaken in an appropriate way. Such journeying would not attain its goal if among its rules of conduct for the soul were something that would result in producing dangers for that person. On the contrary, the goal is always to strengthen the soul, to gather its forces, so that one becomes capable of bearing the soul experiences that one must undergo if one wishes to spiritually see and understand worlds other than that of sensory existence.

In addition, an essential difference between the sensory world and the suprasensory worlds arises due to the fact that in the suprasensory worlds, seeing, perceiving, and comprehending are related to one another differently than in sensory existence. Someone who hears something about a part of the sensory world will have the feeling, with a certain justification, that he can only fully comprehend it by seeing, by perceiving it. We won't be convinced that we have understood a landscape or a painting unless we have seen them for ourselves. The suprasensory worlds can be comprehended completely if, with unbiased powers of judgment, one receives a true description of them. In order to comprehend and experience all the life-supporting, life-fulfilling forces of the spiritual worlds, one needs only the descriptions that are given by those who can see. Only those who are in a position to observe outside of the sensory body can attain real knowledge of such worlds. In the end, descriptions of the world of spirit must always originate from observers of it. However, the knowledge of these worlds that is necessary for soul life is attained through comprehension. And it is entirely possible that someone is himself not able to see into the suprasensory worlds and nevertheless understands these worlds and their characteristics completely – understands them in a way that, under certain conditions, the soul will and must, with full justification, always demand.

Therefore, it is also possible for one to take the means for one's inner contemplation from the store of inner pictures that one has acquired concerning the worlds of spirit. This is the very best kind of subject matter for contemplation; it is the one that leads most surely to the goal. The belief that suggests it to be an obstacle to the acquisition of one's own suprasensory seeing to have first, before acquiring seeing for oneself, obtained knowledge of facts of the spiritual worlds by means of comprehension, does not correspond to reality. The opposite is rather the case. One will more easily and assuredly arrive at seeing when this is preceded by comprehension than when it is not. Whether one contents oneself with comprehension or strives for seeing depends upon whether or not the urge to make observations on one's own has already arisen. If it has arisen, then a person absolutely cannot help but to seek the opportunity to set forth upon his journeying into the suprasensory worlds. – To understand these worlds, however, is something more and more people will yearn for from now on. This is because a true observation of human life shows that human souls, from the present time on, begin to enter a condition in which they *cannot* arrive at the necessary attitude toward life without understanding the suprasensory worlds.

* * *

When the human being has come so far on his soul-journeying that he carries within himself, in the form of memory, all that he calls himself – all that, within sensory existence, he calls his being – and henceforth experiences himself in what he has now attained as a higher 'I', then he becomes capable of spiritually seeing the course of his life extending beyond sensory earthly existence. The fact will then arise before his spiritual gaze that another existence of his self in the spiritual world preceded this current sensory existence – and that it is in this spirit existence that the true causes of the current shaping of sensory existence are to be found.

One becomes acquainted with the fact that *before* this sensory life, into which one entered when one received a sensory body, one had already lived in a purely spiritual way. – What one now is as a human being, with one's various capacities, with one's various drives – one sees all of this prepared in an existence that one had previously lived through in a purely spiritual world. One beholds oneself as a spiritually living being whose existence preceded one's entrance into the sensory world and who has striven to live, as a sensory being, with exactly those capacities and characteristics of soul that one carries with one and has developed since birth. But one would be trapped in error if one were to say, "Why would I have striven to develop capacities and drives in spirit existence that, now that I carry them with me, I do not like at all?" It makes no difference whether or not something pleases the soul in sensory existence. In spirit existence, the soul gives weight to quite different criteria than those to which it will later attach value in sensory existence. The manner of knowing and willing is completely different in each world. When one is in spirit existence, one knows that, for one's development as a whole, one needs a sensory life – one that may then run its course in a way that is unsympathetic or depressing for the soul. And yet one strives for that sensory life because in spirit existence one pays little attention to what one finds sympathetic and comfortable, but concerns oneself solely with what is necessary for the right unfolding of one's own existence.

It is similar with the events of destiny that one encounters in life. Looking at these events, one spiritually sees how, in spirit existence, one oneself prepared what is now sympathetic and also what is unsympathetic, how one brought about the means that cause one to undergo this or that joyful or painful event in sensory existence. Also in this connection, as long as one experiences oneself only in sensory existence, one can find it incomprehensible that one has brought about this or that situation for oneself. And yet, when in the realm of spirit existence, one had what might be called a suprasensory insight that led one to say to oneself: "You must undergo what is painful or unsympathetic to you because only these experiences will bring you a stage further in your overall development." When judging things from the perspective of sensory existence alone, one will never be able to know in what way a concrete earthly life might help an individual to move forward on the path of his overall development.

After having attained knowledge of a spirit existence preceding earthly sensory existence, one will get a glimpse of the reasons why, in spirit existence, one strove for this particular quality and this particular destiny in one's sensory existence. These reasons lead one back to an earlier earthly life that one had lived through in the past. Depending upon how this ran its course, depending on what specific experiences one has had or what capacities one has attained, one strove, during the subsequent spirit existence, to more thoroughly live through experiences that one had only lived through in a meager way and to develop capacities that had still remained undeveloped. For example, while in spirit existence, one experiences an injustice that one had done to another person in such a way that one feels one has thereby disturbed the cosmic world order and that it is necessary, in the course of one's next life, to be present on earth at the same time with that person in order, through one's relation with him, to make good the injustice. – As the soul progresses in its development, its range of vision expands over a series of previous earthly lives. In this way, one succeeds in gaining observation-based knowledge of the true biography of the higher 'I'. One sees that a human being goes through his entire existence by means of repeated earthly lives, and that between these repeated earthly lives are purely spiritual biographies that have a lawful connection with the earthly lives.

In this way, knowledge of repeated earthly lives is brought to the point of actual observation. (Just to avoid the type of misunderstandings that have occurred repeatedly, something should here be mentioned that is presented more precisely in my other works. The entire existence of a human being does not run its course in such a way that life repeats itself forever. A certain number of repetitions take place, which are preceded and followed by quite other forms of existence. The process in its totality manifests as a wisdom-filled development.)

The knowledge that a human being develops through repeated lives can also be gained through reason-based observation of sensory existence. In my books *Theosophy* and *An Outline of Occult Science*, as well as in other shorter works, I tried to provide proof for repeated earthly lives and their interrelations in a form that is characteristic of what is currently practiced in the scientific considerations of present-day evolutionary theory. These works attempted to show how logically consistent thinking and research, when it really takes natural-scientific research to its conclusion, can lead nowhere else than to applying the idea of evolution as formulated in recent times to the case of the human being in such a way that the true essential being, the human soul-individuality, is regarded as something that evolves by passing through repeated earthly lives as well as intervening biographies of a purely spiritual nature. What was sought in these books as proof could naturally be expanded and perfected. However, the opinion cannot appear unjustified that proof in this realm possesses exactly the same scientific validity as what one currently calls natural-scientific proof. There is nothing in the science of the spirit that cannot be supported by means of proof formulated in the very same way as natural-scientific proof. One must nevertheless admit, however, that it is quite obviously much more difficult for spiritual-scientific proof to gain acceptance than it is for proof in the natural sciences. This is not because spiritual-scientific proof lacks rigor but because, when faced with it, one does not feel beneath one's feet the ground of sensory facts that makes it easy to agree with natural-scientific proof. But that has nothing at all to do with the strength of the proof in itself. Whoever is able to compare, impartially and without bias, natural-scientific proof with spiritual-scientific proof given in a natural-scientific manner will easily convince himself that both are of the same value in terms of their strength of proof. Thus, what is affirmed by proof with respect to repeated earthly lives can serve to complement what an observer of the spiritual worlds is able to give, out of his own seeing, concerning the same subject. Both ways are suited to support one another, and this enables one to convince oneself, on the basis of pure comprehension, of the fact that the human biography in its entirety unfolds in repetition. – Here, however, the attempt has been made to show the path that leads beyond comprehension to the suprasensory seeing of this repetition.

# AFTERWORD
(1918)

It may well be clear from what is said in the second of these "meditations" – and it will be recognizable with still greater clarity through what follows – that the path of the soul spoken of in this book rejects in the most decisive way all so-called "clairvoyance" based on pathological or abnormal bodily conditions. All that is of a visionary or mediumistic nature, and all that has its origin in such conditions, is completely ruled out on this path of the soul. Such soul contents emerge from a state of human inner life in comparison to which sense perception and the thinking based upon it represent a higher region. With this very sense perception and thinking, one lives *to a greater degree* in the suprasensory region, and one is *more* independent of the body, than is the case when a disordered bodily organization presents to the soul a deceptive content that, in actual fact, arises from processes that are originally intended to serve the body but instead deviate from their natural tasks in a pathological way, leading to inner pictures that have their foundation neither in outer perceiving nor in an individual activity of will.

Among the soul-processes that reside in ordinary consciousness, it is only *thinking* that can detach itself from perception and lead to independent activity unconditioned by abnormal manifestations of the body. What is here understood by the term "clairvoyant seeing" does not go below this soul condition. It does not descend deeper into organic processes; rather, it rises into regions that *begin* with thinking – with a thinking that is inwardly illuminated by the soul and governed by one's own will. Starting from such self-governed thinking, the soul develops clairvoyant seeing as it is meant here. Thinking is the exemplary model for spiritual seeing. What is described in these "meditations" as such seeing, however, certainly differs in essential ways from mere thinking. And it leads to experiences of suprasensory worlds into which this mere thinking cannot enter. But the life that the soul unfolds in such seeing should nevertheless be no other than that which is developed in thinking. The soul must live in its suprasensory visions and illuminations with the same consciousness with which it lives in a thought, and with which it moves from one thought to another.

The relationship of the soul to these visions is, of course, essentially different from its relationship to ordinary thoughts. Although for the soul the relation of a vision to the reality corresponding to it is similar to how an inner picture of memory relates to a reality that has been experienced and is then remembered by means of this inner picture, what is significant in spiritual seeing is precisely the fact that, during its activity, the power of memory in the soul is entirely inactive. What one has once *inwardly pictured*, one can remember again – even if the inner picture is nothing but a product of fantasy. But what one has experienced in clairvoyant seeing disappears from consciousness in the moment the vision ceases if one has not developed another power of soul in addition to that of spiritual seeing: namely, a power that allows one to re-create in the soul the same conditions of spiritual seeing that led to this vision. One can then remember these conditions and thereby repeat the vision, but one cannot directly remember the vision. As soon as one has acquired the necessary insight into these things, one will find through this insight a means of reliably recognizing that what corresponds to one's vision actually is a reality. Just as one can remember a perception or an experience but in doing so does not undergo the original experience or perception as such, so what remains of the vision for memory does not itself contain the real content of this vision. From this, one can see that the suprasensory reality corresponding to a clairvoyant vision is just as little to be regarded as a mere illusion as is an actual perception in the realm of the senses. People who have not familiarized themselves sufficiently with the nature of the spiritual seeing here described and who judge reports of these things from a merely outer perspective, on the basis of their preconceptions, will easily fall into error here. They think that what arises in clairvoyant consciousness could have to do with the play of fantasy or an interweaving of inner pictures overflowing from the unconscious depths of the soul like vague memories. Those who make such judgments do not know that genuine clairvoyant consciousness lives only in contents of the soul that, by their nature, can never submerge into the organic depths and that, upon their very arising, resist the fate of being caught by any power of memory.

A further distinctive feature of clairvoyant life is that its course differs in important aspects from that of ordinary soul life. In the latter, *practice* and habituation play a fruitful role in human life. Whoever performs a certain act repeatedly, enhances his capacity to perform that act skillfully. What would happen to progress in life and art – and how would any kind of learning be possible – if such increase in human skillfulness could not be attained through practice? But the same is not true of the acquisition of clairvoyant seeing. To have achieved one suprasensory experience does not mean that one is thereby more capable of achieving this experience a second time. Rather, to have experienced it once will cause that experience to elude one. The experience, in a sense, tries to flee from one. Therefore, one has to draw upon specific processes of the soul – processes that will endow the soul with a power greater than that which had first enabled one to achieve this experience, thus allowing one to repeat the experience. This is a source of bitter disappointment for beginners on the soul's path to the suprasensory. It is relatively easy to have initial suprasensory experiences in the course of carrying out exercises that lead to a strengthening of the soul in the sense indicated in this book. At first, then, one may be delighted at the progress one has made. Soon, however, one will notice that experiences of this same kind do not recur. One's soul then feels empty before the suprasensory. The point is that one must clearly realize the following: The efforts that have led one to the first experience will not be effective a second time. Rather, stronger and often quite different efforts are required. – One must bring oneself to see that the laws of suprasensory experiencing are in many cases different from, and sometimes even contrary to, those of physical experience. On the other hand, however, one must be careful not to draw the conclusion that one can know something about suprasensory experiencing by thinking that its processes are always akin to an inversion of the corresponding sensory processes. How things actually stand must be recognized through suprasensory experience in each individual case.

A third characteristic of suprasensory experiencing is that these visions light up before clairvoyant consciousness for only a barely measurable span of time. It could be said that in the moment they appear, they have also already escaped. Consequently, only an immediate awareness, an immediate adjustment of attention, leads one to notice genuine visions. Whoever does not develop among his soul capacities this immediacy of consciousness and immediacy of adjusting one's attention may have visions but will not attain knowledge of them. This is actually the reason why people so widely deny the existence of the suprasensory world. Suprasensory experiencing is in fact much more widespread than people usually think. The interaction between human beings and the spiritual world is, after all, entirely common to all mankind. But the capacity to follow and simultaneously recognize this interaction through the immediate working of one's power of consciousness can only be gained with great effort. One can prepare oneself for this capacity in ordinary life through training oneself, in certain life situations, to form a resolution for action out of a quick survey of what one faces. A person who habitually allows himself, in such life situations, to repeatedly reconsider resolutions that he has made and to constantly hesitate in a way that leads nowhere ("Should I, or shouldn't I?") will be ill-prepared by a life of this nature for the observation of the spiritual world. But a person who, already in this life, manages to develop presence of mind whenever this proves necessary will be able to carry this presence of mind with him into suprasensory experiencing, for which it is an absolute requirement. – If the capacities of suprasensory experiencing were already to reside within one just as one is in ordinary life, then one would be unfit to fulfill one's tasks in the sensory world. One can acquire suprasensory capacities in a beneficial way only when one develops them from out of a healthy life in sensory reality. Whoever believes that one can approach the suprasensory world through turning away from this life, through adopting unusual characteristics, is on an erroneous path. True clairvoyant seeing relates to the healthy processes of ordinary consciousness in the same way as this ordinary consciousness relates to sleep consciousness, whose content arises before the soul in the form of dreams. Just as an unhealthy sleep life disturbs and undermines ordinary consciousness, so healthy clairvoyant seeing cannot build upon the basis of an attitude in ordinary reality that is impractical and hostile toward life. The more firmly one stands in life and the more well-disposed one is toward one's tasks in intellectual, feeling, moral, and social existence, the more one will be able to give rise, in a healthy way, to those soul capacities that will enable one to experience the suprasensory worlds. – The meditations in this book speak of this kind of healthy clairvoyant seeing. One will find nothing that is pathological, or visionary and fantastic in the bad sense, on the path described in these meditations – a path that leads to knowing the suprasensory worlds.

# CITATION NOTES

All citation notes are by the editors of the Chadwick Library.

[1] Rudolf Steiner, *Theosophy: An Introduction to the Suprasensory Knowledge of the World and the Vocation of Man* (New York, NY: Chadwick Library Edition, 2019). *An Outline of Occult Science*, trans. M., H., and L. Monges (Spring Valley, NY: Anthroposophic Press, 1972).

[2] We have chosen to preserve Rudolf Steiner's original paragraphing, as well as his use of the dash between sentences as a way of indicating a sub-paragraph or change of theme within a paragraph.

[3] Rudolf Steiner, *Knowledge of the Higher Worlds: How Is It Achieved?* (London: Rudolf Steiner Press, 1993).

[4] Throughout this book, *Vorstellung* – a key word in German philosophical texts – has generally been translated as "inner picture" or "conception." In certain contexts and in other works of Rudolf Steiner in the Chadwick Library Edition, it may also appear as "inner representation," "mental picture," or "idea," depending upon the judgment of the translating team.

[5] In this text, we have often chosen to translate the German word *schauen* ("to see") as "to see spiritually" or "to spiritually see," as this term designates a mode of seeing that is not of the physical world.

# TWO PUBLISHER'S NOTES

## ON THE SELECTION OF RUDOLF STEINER'S WRITTEN WORKS

A small group, inspired by the work of the late horticulturalist Alan Chadwick, initiated the idea to republish – mostly in new or thoroughly revised English translations – a number of the written works of Rudolf Steiner.

The unifying theme of this edition is that, to this small group, these texts speak most directly of Dr. Steiner.

## ON THE APPROACH TO TRANSLATION AND THE GENDER NEUTRAL QUESTION

Rudolf Steiner generally refers to the individual human being ("der Mensch") in the third person singular form; such references in German are traditionally translated into English using the pronouns "he/his." For a translator preferring an alternative, the pronoun "one," or the phrase "he or she" is an option; but in texts where reflexive references often occur many times within a single sentence, consistently using "one," or "he or she," can present a challenge to the fidelity of the author's intended rhythm or syntax.

An alternative "gender neutral" approach is to replace references to the individual with references to the collective whole (of all human beings). Thus, "he/his" becomes "we/our" or "they/their."

Here, gender neutrality is upheld, but, again, at the expense of the author's chosen form, and more specific identification with "the individual."

The editorial board of the Chadwick Library recognizes that compromise is inherent in each possibility. The editorial board is equally of the view that in some instances the author's direct address to the individual is of a heightened necessity, while in others, a reference to the collective could just as well suffice. We have attempted to find a balance, while at the same time allowing for judgment and freedom for each of the translators.

As was common in his time, Rudolf Steiner used the third person singular grammatical form "he/his" as a neutral term. The pronoun "he/his" was intended, and regularly used, as an expression of neither masculine nor feminine determination; it was understood that grammatical "genus" does not equal gender – as is still widely sensed to be true in the German language today.

This is the sixth volume to be published in the Chadwick Library Edition of Selected Written Works of Rudolf Steiner. This translation is by Julia Selg and Thomas O'Keefe.
Design by Martino Mardersteig in Caslon MM version, setting and printing by Opero in Verona, on Munken Pure paper. Binding by Ruggero Rigoldi in Monza.
Of a total of 850 copies, 750 copies have been bound with leather spines, and 100 have been bound in full leather and numbered 1 to 100.

## VOLUMES PUBLISHED TO DATE

Vol. 1 The Case for Anthroposophy

Vol. 2 Goethean Science: Introductions to Goethe's Natural-Scientific Writings

Vol. 3 Mystics at the Dawn of the Modern Age and Their Relation to the Current Natural-Scientific Paradigm

Vol. 4 The Riddles of Philosophy, Presented in an Outline of Their History, Part I

The Riddles of Philosophy, Presented in an Outline of Their History, Part II

Vol. 5 The Threshold of the Spiritual World

Vol. 6 A Path to Self-Knowledge

Vol. 7 Theosophy

## FORTHCOMING VOLUMES

Christianity as Mystical Fact and the Mysteries of Antiquity

Knowledge of the Higher Worlds and Its Attainment

Esoteric Science: An Outline (three volumes)

The Philosophy of Spiritual Activity